MW01043705

The new ICELANDIC COOKBOOK

All rights reserved. No part of this book may be reproduced
in any form, without the written permission of the publisher.

THE NEW ICELANDIC COOKBOOK
© Mál og menning, Reykjavík 1997
First edition Njála Books 1993
Second printing 1994
Third printing 1997

Printing and binding: in China through Mandarin Offset
Colour separations: Prentmyndastofan
Editor: Atli Vagnsson
Recipes (except traditional dishes): Garðar Agnarsson
Artwork and design: Ragnheiður Kristjánsdóttir
Food photography: Oddur Sigurðsson
Nature photography: Ragnar Axelsson
Oddur Sigurðsson
Páll Imsland
Photo captions: Egill H. Bragason
Translation: Ottó Jónsson
Anna Yates
Front cover: Brunch in the Blue Lagoon photographed by Ragnar Axelsson

ISBN 9979-3-1524-5

The new ICELANDIC COOKBOOK

70 DISHES

Each recipe serves two persons

Mál og menning
Reykjavík 1997

Introduction

What makes Icelandic food special in the culinary world? Is it the raw material obtained from unpolluted natural sources or is it the unsurpassed methods of cooking? The answer is simple. Icelandic food is produced from the best raw materials available: fish from a clean ocean and uncontaminated lakes, meat from animals fed on mountain vegetation, vegetables grown in a climate free from factory smoke and industrial pollution. Icelanders are proud of their unique, natural surroundings. National pride is reflected in the art of cooking where national traditions, based on age-old experience, are manifest. Traditional fish and lamb have formed the staple Icelandic diet. But the Icelanders keep well abreast of the times and have never been tied down by ancient customs. In this century new and fresh currents have pervaded the life of the nation, benefiting the national cuisine in particular. The Icelanders have adopted modern cooking methods and new ways of serving food where old and new form an interesting and often unexpected blend.

This cook book is the first of its kind. Only natural raw materials are used so there are no beef, pork or chicken dishes. The book meets the wishes of the large number of those who read English and want to become acquainted with the Icelandic cuisine for instance after visiting this country. This is not a textbook or a source book on the Icelandic cuisine for chefs.The book is intended for the general reader who wants to have a try at Icelandic cooking. The raw material has been chosen with an eye to its availability abroad.

There is a saying to the effect that if you want to get to know a new nation, one of the best ways is to familiarize yourself with the national food. Eating habits tell us much more than words. The art of food making comes straight from the heart. There is much truth in this as far as Iceland is concerned.

The Icelanders way of thinking is reflected in their cookery. The dishes in the book are not complicated and can be easily prepared if you follow the instructions. The dishes are delicious, beautifully served and not over-elaborate. The Icelandic people love food which is easy to prepare, tastes good and is not too strong or spicy. Natural food from an unspoiled environment is the chosen diet of the people of the country of ice and fire.

Radical changes in the eating habits of the Icelanders have taken place in this century. Yet traditional Icelandic food such as THORRAMATUR, where food is preserved by salting, pickling, smoking and storing in brine, is still very popular.

In the course of time the old Icelandic food is giving way to dishes made from fresh raw material. Much importance is attached to rendering the food as wholesome as possible. Icelanders travel much abroad and have therefore become familiar with the culinary habits of other nations. The foreign influence has partly found expression in the changed eating habits of the nation but the characteristic methods will always remain the foundation of Icelandic cooking.

Icelanders have always consumed milk and

milk products on a larger scale than many other nations. Icelandic dairy products are among the best known in the world today. Icelandic spring water, which during thousands of years has seeped through layers of rock deep down in the earth, is quite free from pollution and additives which contaminate the drinking water of some nations. The pure water plays an important part in making milk products like cheese and butter among the best known. Skyr, which is low in calories and rich in calcium, has a special place among the dairy products and is very popular with foreigners.

In recent decades a great change in the nation´s consumption of meat has occurred. Much more pork and chicken are now being consumed. Accordingly new recipes have appeared in accordance with national taste.

The import of vegetables and fruit has spurred Icelanders today to grow all vegetables themselves in well-equipped greenhouses many of which are heated with geothermal energy. One of the first things observed by foreign tourists in Iceland is geothermal energy and the hot springs. The utilization of energy from the bowels of the earth for the production of vegetables close to the Arctic Circle (vegetables which otherwise would not grow except in much more southerly countries) is characteristic of the nation´s way of thinking. This policy is also in agreement with the Icelandic people´s determination to be self-sufficient in as many fields as possible and to utilize technology to the utmost.

Wild game is one of the raw materials in greatest demand in international cuisine. The same applies to Iceland where ptarmigan takes first place. It is also justifiable to maintain that the Icelandic mountain lamb is almost wild game. The lambs roam the uplands the whole summer, feeding on mountain vegetation and drinking pure water from brooks and springs, which is unknown in many places of the world. For these reasons the Icelandic lamb is particularly tasty and natural for all kinds of cooking, a fact best known to the Icelanders themselves.

Discussing Iceland necessitates a mention of the pillar of the nation´s economy, i. e. its fish.The Icelanders catch numerous kinds of fish and marine animals. For centuries only few species of fish were caught but in the last few decades the variety in fishing and processing has increased by leaps and bounds. Simultaneously the nation has learnt to cook new species and given older dishes of fish a face lift. Traditional methods of preservation like the salting and smoking of fish is still practised on a large scale and enjoys great popularity. However, nothing can replace fresh fish or fish frozen at sea.The Icelanders are indefatigable in exploring new avenues in the preparation of fish, and this book will afford the reader many interesting recipes.

The readers of the book are urged to acquaint themselves with innovations in Icelandic cooking and not to hesitate to try the recipes in the book. The dishes will prove successful when the best raw material of the world is available and the recipes strictly adhered to.

Bon appetit!

Atli Vagnsson

The Chef

Garðar Agnarsson has worked with many of Iceland's finest chefs since graduating from the Icelandic Hotel and Catering School in 1987. He keeps up with the latest trends in international cuisine. Although every branch of cuisine is at his fingertips, his particular passion is for fish cookery. We feel that Garðar Agnarsson is a worthy representative of the younger generation of Icelanders, who are creating Iceland's own nouvelle cuisine.

The Photographers

Oddur Sigurðsson, geologist and glaciologist, works for the National Energy Authority of Iceland. His nature photographs have been published in many books and periodicals. He took all the photographs of the dishes in the book, as well as several of the nature photographs.

Ragnar Axelsson, one of the best-known photographers in Iceland, works for the country's main newspaper, Morgunblaðið. He has won prizes for his photography, and his work has been published in such prestigious plublications as National Geographic, Time, Life and Stern.

Páll Imsland holds a doctoral degree in geology and works as a research geologist at the University of Iceland. He has been an active photographer of Icelandic nature for over twenty years.

Contents

Hors D'oeuvres

Soups

Fish

Lamb

Wild Game

Desserts

Traditional dishes

Thorramatur

A tasty hors d´oeuvre is appetizing and indispensible on festive occasions. The hors d´oeuvre should be rather simple but of an appetizing appearance and texture. The time it takes to decorate hors d´oeuvres is not wasted. Icelandic hors d´oeuvres are chiefly based on shellfish, lobster, shrimps or scallops. Smoked or marinated salmon is also popular. All kinds of wild game paté have come to the fore recently, as well as seafood paté. The Icelandic raw material affords numerous possibilities of preparing hors d´oeuvres, the question being only where to begin and end.

RAX

Hors D'oeuvres

Icelandic flora have adapted to the rugged environment of the uplands over thousands of years. Saxifrage thrives on rock scoured by glacial ice, where no other plant can grow.

LOBSTER MOUSSE

200 g (7 oz) shelled lobster
1 egg
3/4 dl (3 fl oz 3/8 cup) cream
1 tsp ginger
1 tbsp chopped oregano
1/2 tsp curry powder
salt
pepper
4 leaves lettuce
4 blackcurrants (garnish)

Sauce:
100 g (3 1/2 oz) beetroot
1/2 dl (2 fl oz 1/4 cup) fish stock
1/2 dl (2 fl oz 1/4 cup) cream
cornflour

Trim the lobster. Put in a mixer with ginger, currypowder, oregano, salt and pepper. Mix for 2-3 seconds. Add the cream and mix for 5 seconds. Gently beat in the egg. Wrap in a plastic film, roll up and tie the ends. Boil in a pot for 7-8 minutes at low heat. Cool in the fridge. Peel beetroot and cut into small cubes. Put fish stock in a pot with beetroot and boil for 2-3 minutes. Season with salt and pepper. Add cream, boil for 1-2 minutes. Thicken with cornflour and boil for a minute. Put the sauce on the plate and lettuce leaves on top. Slice lobster mousse and arrange on the lettuce leaves. Garnish with blackcurrants to taste.

PÁLL

TROUT TARTARE WITH CAVIAR

160 g (5 1/3 oz) fresh trout, skinned and boned
juice of 1/4 lemon
1 tsp olive oil
1 tsp red onion
1 tsp sage
1/4 tsp horseradish
salt
pepper
2 tsp chives
4 tbsp natural yoghurt
1 tbsp lemon juice
lumpfish caviar

Chop the trout fillet finely. Mix together the juice of 1/4 lemon, 1 tsp olive oil with the chopped red onion, sage and grated horse radish. Place the trout in the marinade and mix well and season with salt and pepper.

Sauce:

Cut the chives into the yoghurt and add the lemon juice. Serve with yoghurt sauce and lumpfish caviar.

MARINATED SALMON AND OCEAN PERCH WITH AVOCADO

120 g (4 oz) salmon, skinned and boned
80 g (2 1/2 oz) ocean perch fillets, skinned and boned
1/2 avocado
2 tsp lemon juice
1 shallot
a dash of cayenne pepper
1 tbsp natural yoghurt
1 tsp grated lemon peel
juice of 1/4 lemon
juice of 1/4 red grapefruit
2 tsp apple juice
1/4 dl (1 fl oz 1/8 cup) peanut oil
salt
pepper
6 segments grapefruit
1 tbsp mint

Separate the grapefruit segments. Marinade: mix the juice of lemon and grapefruit with the apple juice, peanut oil, lemon peel and mint and season with salt and pepper. Cut the fish sideways into very thin slices. Marinate for 10 minutes. Purée the avocado in a mixer together with lemon peel, 2 tsp lemon juice, shallot and yoghurt. Season with cayenne and salt. Arrange the fish with the grapefruit segments and avocado purée on a plate.

The work of fishermen involves careful preparation, on land and at sea, building upon the craftsmanship of generations. Netmending is often undertaken by aged seamen, who like to feel they remain in touch with the sea.

RAX

LOBSTER WITH LIME

160 g (5 oz) shelled lobster
2 stalks green asparagus
1 lime peel
2 tbsp kidney beans
1 tomato
1/2 carrot
50 g (2 oz) butter
1/2 dl (2 fl oz 1/4 cup) white wine
oil for frying
salt
pepper

Wash the lobster. Boil asparagus in lightly salted water for 1 minute. Cool. Cut carrots in strings. Boil kidney beans. Slice tomatoes. Cut peel from lime into strings. Fry lobster, asparagus and carrots in hot oil for about 20 seconds and season with salt and pepper. Add kidney beans and tomatoes during the last five seconds. Place on a plate. Put the peel in a pan, pour in the white wine and add a dash of salt. Add cold butter, stir well and sprinkle over the dish.

Could anyone live in such a place without being overcome by the magnificence of nature, and feeling, at the same time, that folklore about trolls and elves may not be all imagination?

A geyser spouts boiling water and steam dozens of metres into the air. The noise, the overwhelming power from beneath the earth, clouds of steam and a fine spray of hot water, the odour of sulphur, combine to make for unforgettable memories.

SMOKED SALMON WITH PRAWN SALAD

10 slices of smoked salmon
200 g (7 oz) prawns
1/2 tsp chopped ginger
30 g (1 oz) iceberg lettuce finely cut
20 g (2/3 oz) leek, the white part thinly sliced
2 tbsp diced red bell pepper
2 slices of toast

Sauce:
2 tbsp sour cream
1 tbsp ketchup
1/4 tsp cayenne
salt
pepper

Mix the prawns, lettuce, ginger, bell pepper and the leek with the sauce. Spread the whole mixture on the slices of salmon. Serve with bread.

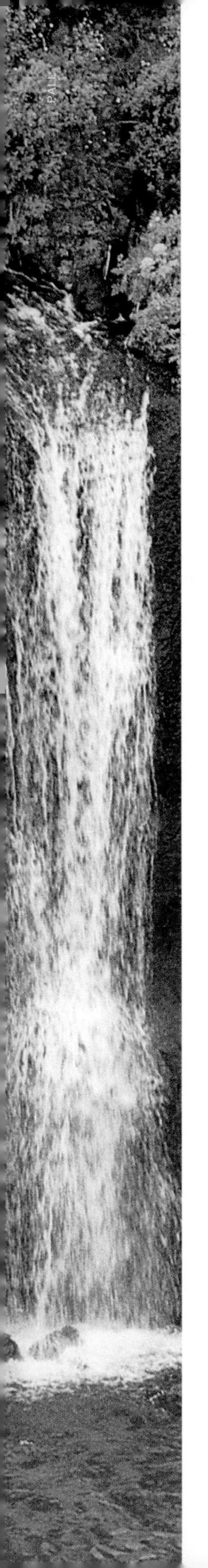

MARINATED SALMON WITH ANISEED

200 g (7 oz) salmon fillets unskinned
50 g (2 oz) freshly ground salt
20 g (2/3 oz) freshly ground pepper
50 g (2 oz) brown sugar
2 tbsp dill
4 tbsp aniseed
1 dl (3 1/2 fl oz 1/2 cup) cous cous
1/2 dl (2 fl oz 1/4 cup) fish stock
4 tsp olive oil
1/4 cucumber
1 tomato
1 tbsp parsley
salt
pepper

Mix together the salt, pepper, brown sugar, dill and aniseed. Spread it on the salmon fillets and leave at room temperature for about 10-12 hours. Boil the cous cous in the fish stock for 3-4 minutes. Pour into a bowl and loosen with a fork. Remove the juice of the tomato. Cut the tomato and the cucumber into small cubes. Chop the parsley. Mix with the cous cous and the oil. Season with salt and pepper. Cut the salmon into thin slices and serve with cous cous and lettuce.

Hraunfossar. Crystal-clear spring water tumbles down the rock-face from beneath a rugged lava field dotted with shrubs and trees. Many Icelandic poets have composed verse about the beauty of their country, and no wonder.

Icelanders are used to the vicissitudes of their climate, and cheerfully get out to push a car out of a snowdrift. After all, this is Iceland.

SCALLOPS WITH SAFFRON

180 g (6 oz) scallops
1 red onion
40 g (1 1/2 oz) leek
1 shallot
1/8 tsp saffron
1/2 dl (2 fl oz 1/4 cup) white wine
1/4 dl (1 fl oz 1/8 cup) cream
2 tbsp butter
salt
pepper
oil for frying

Cut red onion and leek. Chop shallot and tenderize in oil. Add white wine and the saffron and reduce by half. Pour in the cream and boil for a moment. Add cold butter and season with salt and pepper. Sautée scallops and vegetables. Arrange on a plate and pour the sauce around.

RAX

Eruption of Mt Krafla on 8 October 1980. The volcano had erupted from time to time since 1975. Icelanders are accustomed to volcanic activity in the "land of ice and fire".

PÁLL

MARINATED LAMB WITH YOGHURT SAUCE

180 g (6 oz) best end of lamb
2 tbsp salt
2 tbsp brown sugar
1 tsp black pepper
3 tbsp sesame seeds
1/4 dl (1 fl oz 1/8 cup) cognac
1 tbsp thyme
1 tbsp oregano
2 tbsp mango chutney
4 tbsp natural yoghurt
cucumber
2 tsp lemon juice

Sauce: roast in a pan, 1 tbsp sesame seeds and mix with the yoghurt and the lemon juice. Set aside. Make a marinade of the salt, brown sugar, crushed black pepper, 2 tbsp of sesame seeds, cognac, thyme, oregano and 1 tbsp of mango chutney. Spread it over the lamb and press well. Let stand for at least 8 hours and turn the meat occasionally. Cut the meat into thin slices. Serve with the yoghurt sauce, 1 tbsp mango chutney and shredded cucumber.

Soups

The Icelanders have made soups since the settlement of Iceland, making use of traditional ingredients. Meat and fish soups occupy a prominent place but in recent times vegetable soups have become popular. The increasing variability of seafood has afforded greater possibilities of preparing new soups. Icelandic cooks have done their utmost to introduce innovations in this field. Nothing can replace a soup before the main course. The aroma of a delicious soup puts everyone in a festive mood.

RAX

RAX

TRADITIONAL MEAT SOUP

(kjötsúpa)

400 g (14 oz) lamb, best end of neck
7.5 dl (1 1/3 pt 3 1/4 cup) water
1 onion
2 potatoes
200 g (7 oz) swedes/rutabaga
200 g (7 oz) carrots
1 tbsp rice
1 tbsp herbs
1 tbsp salt

Put meat in cold water, add salt and bring to the boil. Remove froth and reduce temperature. Boil at low heat for 45- 50 minutes. In the meantime, peel vegetables and cut into fairly large pieces. After 20 minutes of boiling add vegetables, rice and herbs. Serve meat in the soup or separately.

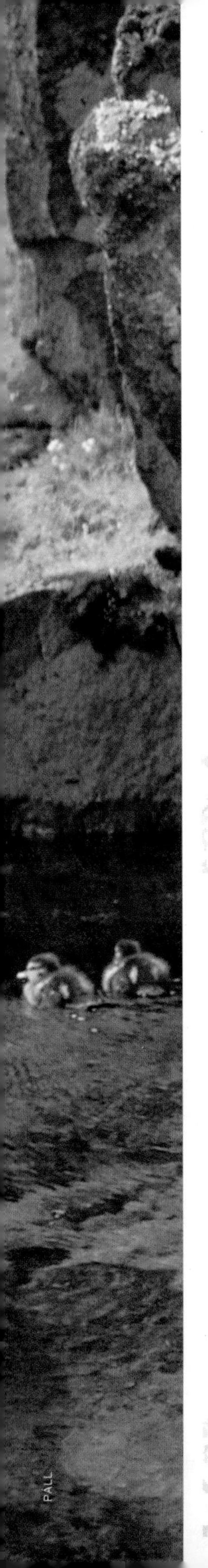

FISH SOUP DELICACY

1 1/2 dl (5 fl oz 5/8 cup) fish stock
1 1/2 dl (5 fl oz 5/8 cup) cream
1/2 dl (2 fl oz 1/4 cup) white wine
1 tsp mild curry
1/4 tsp turmeric
8 scallops
8 shrimps
4 small lobster tails
60 g (2 oz) salmon
30 g (1 oz) haddock
30 g (1 oz) halibut
1 tbsp butter

Thicken fish stock suitably. Melt butter in a pot. Add turmeric and curry and stir, do not burn. Pour white wine in the pot and reduce by half. Add the fish stock, then cream and simmer for 1-2 minutes. Put in the soup scallops, halibut, salmon, haddock and lobster tails. The shrimps are added last. Serve with bread.

PALL

A mallard and her ducklings in spring. Small flowers bloom, and vegetation revives in gentle tints of green. The Icelanders give the spring a warm welcome each year, as nature makes her yearly recovery after the rigours of winter.

RAX

HALIBUT SOUP

200 g (7oz) halibut
2 dl (7 fl oz 7/8 cup) fish stock
1 egg yolk
1/2 dl (2 fl oz 1/4 cup) cream
5 prunes

Boil the halibut in fish stock with prunes. Remove fish from bones. Thicken fish stock without the prunes. Sieve the stock. Stir together egg yolk and cream and add to stock. The soup must not boil. Cut halibut in pieces and place in the soup together with the prunes.

Fish

Iceland boasts the most abounding fishing grounds in the world. However, it is not the quantity alone that makes the fish important to the nation. Icelandic fish is world famous for its quality. Fresh fish and fish frozen at sea is an unparalleled raw material, not to mention the salmon and freshwater fish which thousands of anglers flock to catch every year, some of them coming from distant parts of the world. There is no end to methods of preparing fish and here are some interesting recipes that make your mouth water. Icelanders have used various methods of curing fish and preparing dishes from it. Fish is salted, smoked, fermented, marinated and dried. All these are old, traditional methods of curing intended to lengthen the storage life of the fish. Fresh fish is popular both boiled, fried, deepfried, grilled or baked in an oven. Herring has become popular in this century with its inexhaustible possibilities of cooking like other kinds of fish. In the old days the whole fish was used even in surprising ways. Shoes were made from the skin of catfish and sewing needles from haddock bone. Shark was fermented, buried in sandy beaches and sometimes kept there for years on end before being consumed. It is easy to take one´s friends by pleasant surprise with gorgeous Icelandic dishes.

Capelin and more capelin - millions of the tiny fish fill the ship's hold. The crew allow themselves a break for some fishy horseplay, before setting sail again, in search of yet more capelin.

OCEAN PERCH WITH GINGER AND OLIVES

400 g (14 oz) red ocean perch fillets
30 g (1 oz) fresh ginger
10 black olives
1 dl (3 1/2 fl oz 1/2 cup) rosé wine
2 shallots
1 dl (3 1/2 fl oz 1/2 cup) fish stock
100 g (3 1/2 oz) butter
oil for frying
bell pepper
parsley
salt
pepper

To make the sauce: Peel the ginger and chop finely. Chop the olives. Chop the shallots and fry until soft. Add the rosé wine, reduce by one third by simmering and add fish stock and cold pieces of butter and let simmer some more. Add salt and pepper to taste. Now fry the fish fillets on both sides in oil at a high temperature. Add the ginger and olives after the fish has been turned in the pan. Season with a pinch of salt. Spread the plate with the sauce. Place the fish on the sauce and the ginger and olives on top of the fish. Sprinkle the pieces of bell peppers and chopped parsley over it.

HALIBUT CHEEKS WITH SOYA-TOMATO SAUCE

450 g (1 lb halibut cheeks)
2 tbsp oil for frying
1/2 zucchini, yellow
1/2 zucchini, green
2 gherkins
2 mushrooms
1 small bell pepper
1 1/2 dl (5 fl oz 5/8 cup) soya sauce
3 tsp ketchup
5 drops Tabasco
100 g (3 1/2 oz) butter
salt
pepper

Heat the oven to 180°C (350°F). Chop vegetables coarsely. Fry the fish on each side in a pan. Put the fish aside. Put the vegetables in the pan and fry. Mix together in a pot the soya sauce, the ketchup and the Tabasco and bring to the boil. Place the fish in the oven. Remove the vegetables from the pan and put aside. Pour the sauce from the pot into the pan, add 100 g of cold butter and stir well. Place the sauce on a plate, then the vegetables and finally the fish.

RAX

SAUTÉED SCALLOPS WITH SMOKED SALMON AND ALMONDS

400 g (14 oz) scallops
50 g (2 oz) smoked salmon
30 g (1 oz) almond flakes
1 dl (3 1/2 fl oz 1/2 cup) white wine
2 dl (7 fl oz 7/8 cup) cream
1 tsp cornflour
150 g (5 oz) puff pastry
1 egg yolk
salt
pepper
2 sprigs chervil
oil for frying

Spread the puff pastry with the egg yolk and cool for 1/2 hour. Bake at 180°C (350°F) for 15-18 minutes. Cut smoked salmon into pieces. Pour oil in a deep pan. Heat well. Fry the scallops rapidly for 15 seconds. Remove from the pan. Pour the white wine into the pan with the cream and allow to simmer for a minute. Thicken with cornflour. Roast the almonds in another pan and add to the sauce together with the salmon and the scallops. Season with salt and pepper. Fill each pastry bun with a layer of the mixture of ingredients. Serve with green salad of your choice.

Rural peace: rugged crags, picturesque old buildings and a horse - man's most useful servant for a thousand years - epitomize the Icelander's idyllic image of the countryside.

RAX

FRIED HERRING

400 g (14 oz) fresh herring fillets
2 tsp olive oil
2 tbsp redwine vinegar
5 olives in brine
2 tsp capers
4 tbsp chopped bell peppers (various colours)
1 tbsp chopped parsley
2 tbsp chopped onion
salt
pepper

Fry the herring in oil in a pan until the fillets are crisp with a golden colour. Season with salt and pepper. Fry the vegetable mixture in olive oil for 10-15 seconds and add the redwine vinegar. Sprinkle the liquid from the mixture over the fillets. Cover the fillets with the vegetables.

In the early years of the 20th century, most Icelandic houses were built of wood; though small, they were cosy and welcoming. The steeply-sloping roofs prevent snow collecting and causing damage to the structure.

RAX

LOBSTER TAILS WITH CAMEMBERT CHEESE

18-22 lobster tails according to size
1/2 camembert cheese
1 dl (3 1/2 fl oz 1/2 cup) cream
2 tsp chopped basil
1/2 dl (2 fl oz 1/4 cup) white wine
bread crumbs
salt
pepper

Cut the lobster tails lengthwise through the shell and unfold. Cut the cheese in thin slices. Combine white wine, cream, basil and cheese in a mixer. Season the tails with salt and pepper. Spread the paste on the lobster and sprinkle with bread crumbs. Grill in oven for 2-3 minutes. Serve with bread.

Wind-drying is one of the oldest and most traditional ways of preserving foods. Iceland sells thousands of tons of stockfish to tropical countries every year. The Icelanders' own favourite, "harðfiskur", is first dried, and then softened by hammering.

FRIED SALTFISH WITH GARLIC AND CHILLIES

400 g (14 oz) saltfish fillets
2 potatoes
6 cloves garlic
2 red chillies
2 green chillies
2 tbsp parsley
1 tbsp butter
1 tbsp oil for frying
2 dl (7 fl oz 7/8 cup) tomato juice
2 cl (0.8 fl oz 1/9 cup) white wine vinegar
chives

Cut the garlic cloves in two. Slice the onions and the chillies. Chop the parsley. Fry the saltfish and the potato slices in the oil and reduce heat. Sautée the garlic and the chilies. Add butter. Pour in the vinegar and the tomato juice. Arrange the potatoes on the plate and the fish on top. Pour the chillie and garlic sauce round the fish and garnish with the chives.

ODDUR

ORANGE ROUGHY WITH HAZELNUT BUTTER

400 g (14 oz) fillets of orange roughy
5o g (2 oz) hazelnut flakes
1 dl (3 1/2 fl oz 1/2 cup) white wine
125 g (4 1/2 oz) butter
salt
pepper
2 tbsp oil

Slice the fillets thinly and dry with paper. Pour the oil into a pan and heat. Place the slices in the pan and fry on both sides and take them from the pan. Keep in the oven at a low temperature. Put about 20 g of the butter in the pan and spread the nut flakes over it. Stir until nicely brown. Add the white wine and season with salt and pepper to taste. Reduce by half by simmering. Add the rest of the butter in small pieces and stir well. Place the fish on a plate and pour the hazelnut butter over it.

SALTFISH ON AUBERGINE

400 g (14 oz) saltfish fillets
1 red onion
1 aubergine
2 mangetout beans
1/4 leek
1 egg
1 dl (3 1/2 fl oz 1/2 cup) soya oil
garlic oil for frying
salt
pepper
chervil for garnishing

Cut the fish into pieces. Set aside. Purée leek in a mixer. Add the egg and then the soya oil, salt and pepper. Cut the aubergine and the red onion into slices. Cut the mangetouts in strings. Fry the aubergine, red onion and the mangetout beans in the garlic oil together with the fish. Place the aubergine on a plate topped with the fish and the onion. Add the cold leek sauce and the mangetouts. Garnish with chervil.

RAX

A roof close to Nature. Huts like this were painstakingly built of stone, to offer emergency shelter to those who travelled over mountain and heathland.

BARBECUED CATFISH

400 g (14 oz) catfish
150 g (5 oz) butter (soft)
1 tbsp dill
juice of 1/2 lemon
salt
pepper
your favorite barbecue sauce

Put the butter into a bowl. Add chopped dill and the lemon juice and season with just a little salt and pepper. Stir well and cool. If you intend to use salad, prepare it now. The fish does not have to be rolled in flour. The grill must be sufficiently hot. First grill for 4-5 minutes, then turn it over and grill the other side for 4-5 minutes. Finally spread on the barbecue sauce sparingly. Place catfish fillets on a tray. Cut the spiced butter from the bowl into thin slices and lay them on the fish.

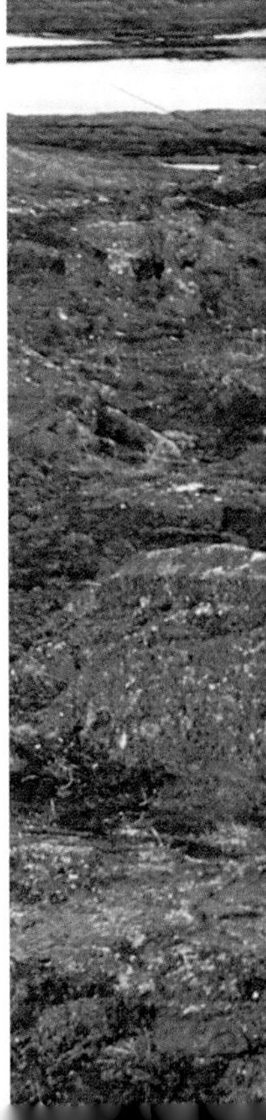

COD WITH CITRUS FRUITS AND NUTS (EN PAPILLOTE)

A light wholesome dish for the outdoor grill or the oven

400 g (14 oz) cod fillet with the skin
2 sheets grease-proof paper
1 lemon
1 orange
1 red grapefruit
10 pecan nuts
10 pistachio nuts
3 dl (1/2 pt 1 1/4 cup) fruit juice
salt
cornflour

Cut the rind from the fruit and detach the leaves. Place the fillet on a sheet of grease-proof paper and salt a little. Arrange some of the fruit neatly on the fillet and sprinkle the crushed nuts over it. Squeeze the juice from the rest of the fruit into a pot. Heat the juice and thicken it with just a little cornflour. Put aside.

Fold the grease-proof paper tightly over the fish and tie if necessary. Bake on an outdoor grill or in an oven for about 8-10 minutes. Open the bag and sprinkle with the juice. Most enjoyable when eaten piping hot straight from the paper.

Seljalandsfoss. A human being feels very small, confronted with the power and beauty of this thundering cascade.

In winter, fish can be caught through the ice on many of Iceland's lakes. On Lake Mývatn in midwinter, an angler has cut a hole in the ice, and is angling for trout. His four-footed companion, an Iceland Dog, is the pure-bred representative of a unique breed.

RAX

FRIED TROUT

2 x 300 g (2 x 11 oz) trout
2 red onions, small
4 tbsp sliced leek
lettuce
30 g (1 oz) bacon
50 g (2 oz) mushrooms
1 dl (3 1/2 oz 1/2 cup) red wine
1 dl (3 1/2 fl oz 1/2 cup) beef stock
150 g (5 oz) butter
salt
pepper
olive oil

Wash the fish and dry it. Cut each onion in four. Slice the mushrooms and cut the bacon into small pieces. Fry the bacon without oil in a frying pan. Then add the onions and mushrooms. Simmer for a while. Add the red wine and reduce to 2/3 by simmering. Pour in the beef stock and keep just below boiling point for a few minutes. Heat the oven to 160°C (325°F). Heat another pan and season the trout. Fry to a golden colour, about three minutes each side. Add 50 g of clarified butter to the pan and place it in the oven. Add 100 g of cold butter to the sauce. Do not boil after that. Serve with fried leek and lettuce.

SALTFISH WITH WARM SALAD

400 g (14 oz) saltfish
8 green olives
8 black olives
1/2 zucchini, green
4 cloves of garlic
6 mangetout beans
10 g (1/3 oz) cashew nuts
1 tomato
1 red onion
1/2 bell pepper
2 mushrooms
1 apple
1 lollo rosso lettuce
1/2 spring onion
40 g (1 1/2 oz) ginger
2 cl (0.8 fl oz 1/9 cup) white wine vinegar
4 cl (1.1 fl oz 1/8 cup) olive oil

Cut the saltfish into large chunks. Chop the vegetables coarsely except for lollo rosso. Sautée the vegetables except for lollo rosso, and mix well. Season with white wine vinegar and olive oil. Fry the salt cod in oil. Place lollo rosso leaves in a circle on the plate. Arrange the vegetables neatly on the plate and place the cod on top of it.

Laugahraun. Much of Iceland is covered with lava from many volcanic eruptions over the centuries. Moss gradually takes root in the lavafield, spreading out like a rich green carpet, and softening the jagged edges of the lava.

SALTFISH WITH GARLIC AND TOMATO SAUCE

400 g (14 oz) saltfish fillets
4 tomatoes
1/2 dl (2 fl oz 1/4 cup) tomato juice
4 cloves of garlic
1 onion
2 tbsp parsley
6 small potatoes
1 small swede, rutabaga
8 haricots
6 baby corn
salt
pepper
oil for frying

After boiling the tomatoes in lightly salted water for 10-15 seconds remove them and place in iced water. Skin the tomatoes and cut into pieces. Set aside. Pour some oil into a pan and heat while chopping onion, garlic and parsley. Sautée in the pan, then add the tomatoes and the tomato juice. Season with a pinch of salt and pepper. Simmer for about 30 minutes with the lid on. Stir occasionally. Chop the vegetables into even pieces and boil lightly. Boil the salt cod for 3-4 minutes. Put sauce on a plate, then fish and finally the vegetables. To save time, canned tomatoes may be used.

RAX

RAX

LEMON SOLE ROLLS

400 g (14 oz) lemon sole fillets
50 g (2 oz) wild mushrooms
50 g (2 oz) fresh spinach leaves
50 g (2 oz) butter
2 tbsp oil
salt
pepper
Sauce:
1/2 onion
1/2 dl (2 fl oz) white wine
50 g (2 oz) blue cheese
1 dl (3 1/2 fl oz 1/2 cup) cream
100 g (3 1/2 oz) spaghetti
1 tbsp oil for frying
1 tsp coarse salt

Wash and dry the spinach leaves. Cut the mushrooms. Sautée the spinach leaves in oil and season with salt and pepper. Fry the mushrooms in butter seasoned with salt. Set aside. Bone the fillets of lemon sole and season with salt and pepper. Boil the spaghetti and cool. Chop the onion and fry in the butter until soft. Pour in the wine, followed by the cheese and finally the cream. Allow to simmer and season with salt and pepper. Arrange the spinach and the mushrooms on the fillets and roll them up. Pack the rolls tightly in a plastic film and tie the ends. Boil the fish for 10-12 minutes at a low temperature. Pour the sauce over the spaghetti and heat. The spaghetti and the sauce are brought on a plate with the fish on top of it. Serve the fish on a bed of spaghetti and sauce.

RAX

CATFISH IN A COAT OF SPICE

This simple and easy dish affords a variety of possibilities according to your taste. Other types of fish can be used with different kinds of spices and pasta.

400 g (14 oz) catfish fillets
2 eggs
2 tsp chopped parsley
1/2 tsp tarragon
1/4 tsp thyme
1/4 tsp sage
1/4 tsp basil
1/4 tsp dill
1/4 tsp rosemary
Butter for frying
Choose pasta according to taste
2 carrots
6 mushrooms
4 baby corn
2 mangetout beans
1 dl (3 1/2 fl oz 1/2 cup) cream
1 dl (3 1/2 fl oz 1/2 cup) beer
salt
pepper
20 g (2/3 oz) flour

Cut the vegetables into small pieces. Boil the pasta. Skin and bone the fish. Cut into suitable pieces. Chop herbs and mix with the beaten eggs. Sautée vegetables in a pan. Pour the beer into it followed by the cream. Simmer at a low temperature, adding some salt and pepper. Meanwhile, melt a little butter in a pan. Roll the fish in flour and then in the egg-spice mixture. Place the fish in the pan, add a pinch of salt and fry until nicely brown. Add pasta to the sauce. Serve the fish with vegetable sauce.

HADDOCK WITH CHEESE AND GRAPES

2 x 200 g (2 x 7 oz) haddock tails
50 g (2 oz) brie cheese
1 egg
100 g (3 1/2 oz) flour
1/4 dl (1 fl oz 1/8 cup) milk
100 g (3 1/2 oz) bread crumbs
1/2 l (18 fl oz) oil for deep frying
10 black grapes
20 cashew nuts, shelled
1/2 dl (1 fl oz 1/8 cup) red wine
100 g (3 1/2 oz) butter
salt
pepper

Press the fish lightly with your palm. Cut the cheese in thin slices and arrange them on the fish. Roll up the haddock. Beat the egg in a bowl, add milk and whisk together. Roll fish in flour, then in the egg mixture and finally in the bread crumbs. Now the rolls should be completely covered with crumbs. If not, repeat the dipping without more flour. Cut the grapes in halves and remove the stones. Heat the oven to 100°C (200°F). Deepfry the rolls to a golden colour. Remove from pot and place them on the oven rack. Roast the nuts in 1 tsp of butter. Add red wine and reduce by half by simmering. Season with salt and pepper. Add cold butter and finally the grapes. Serve.

HALIBUT IN PUFF PASTRY WITH SPINACH

300 g (11 oz) halibut
250 g (9 oz) puff pastry
50 g (2 oz) frozen spinach
1 dl (3 1/2 fl oz 1/2 cup) cream
30 g (1 oz) smoked salmon
salt
pepper
1 egg

Sauce:
1 yellow bell pepper
1/2 dl (2 fl oz 1/4 cup) milk
1/2 dl (2 fl oz 1/4 cup) cream
1 dl (3 1/2 fl oz 1/2 cup) white wine
cornflour for thickening
salt to taste

Roll out the pastry and cool. Cut the halibut into 3 cm (1 inch) pieces and dry carefully. Boil spinach and cream together in a pot until it begins to thicken. Purée in a mixer, add the smoked salmon and a dash of salt and pepper. Cool. Cut the pastry. To make the bottom, cut a smaller circle, and a larger one for the top. Place the halibut on the bottom circle adding a little salt. Spread the edge of the pastry with egg yolk, mixed with water. Cover the halibut with a thin layer of the spinach purée. Then place the top circle and press the edges of the pastry circles with a fork. Garnish with the remaining pastry. Bake at 200°C (400°F) for 10-12 minutes.

Sauce:
Purée the bell pepper in a mixer. Place a sieve on a pot and pour in the pepper mash and press the juice from it into the pot. Add milk and cream and bring to the boil. Thicken with cornflour and add salt and white wine to taste.

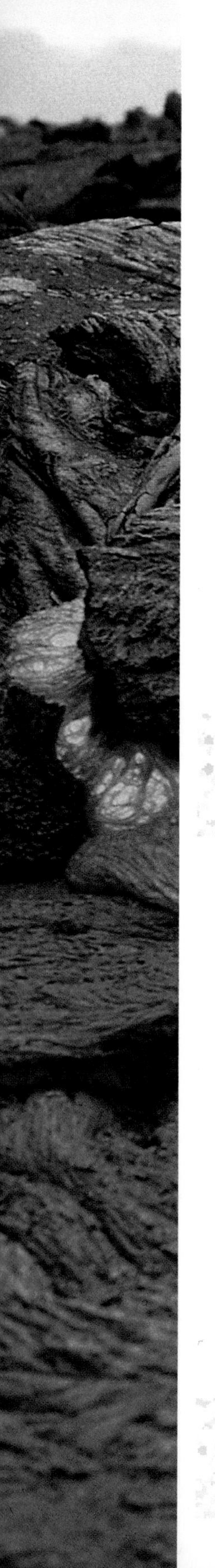

GRILLED MONKFISH TAILS

2 monkfish tails 300 g (11 oz) each tail with the bone
juice of 1/2 lemon
10 g (1/3 oz) fresh chopped herbs: parsley, basil, mint, thyme, tarragon
1 clove crushed garlic
ground pepper
salt

Remove all skin from fish. Pour the mixture of the lemon juice, the herbs and the garlic over the fish and set aside for 40 minutes. Remove the tails from the spice marinad and season with salt and pepper. Grill both sides for 5-6 minutes each. Place on a plate and serve with tomato salad, fresh salad and baked potatoes.

ODDUR

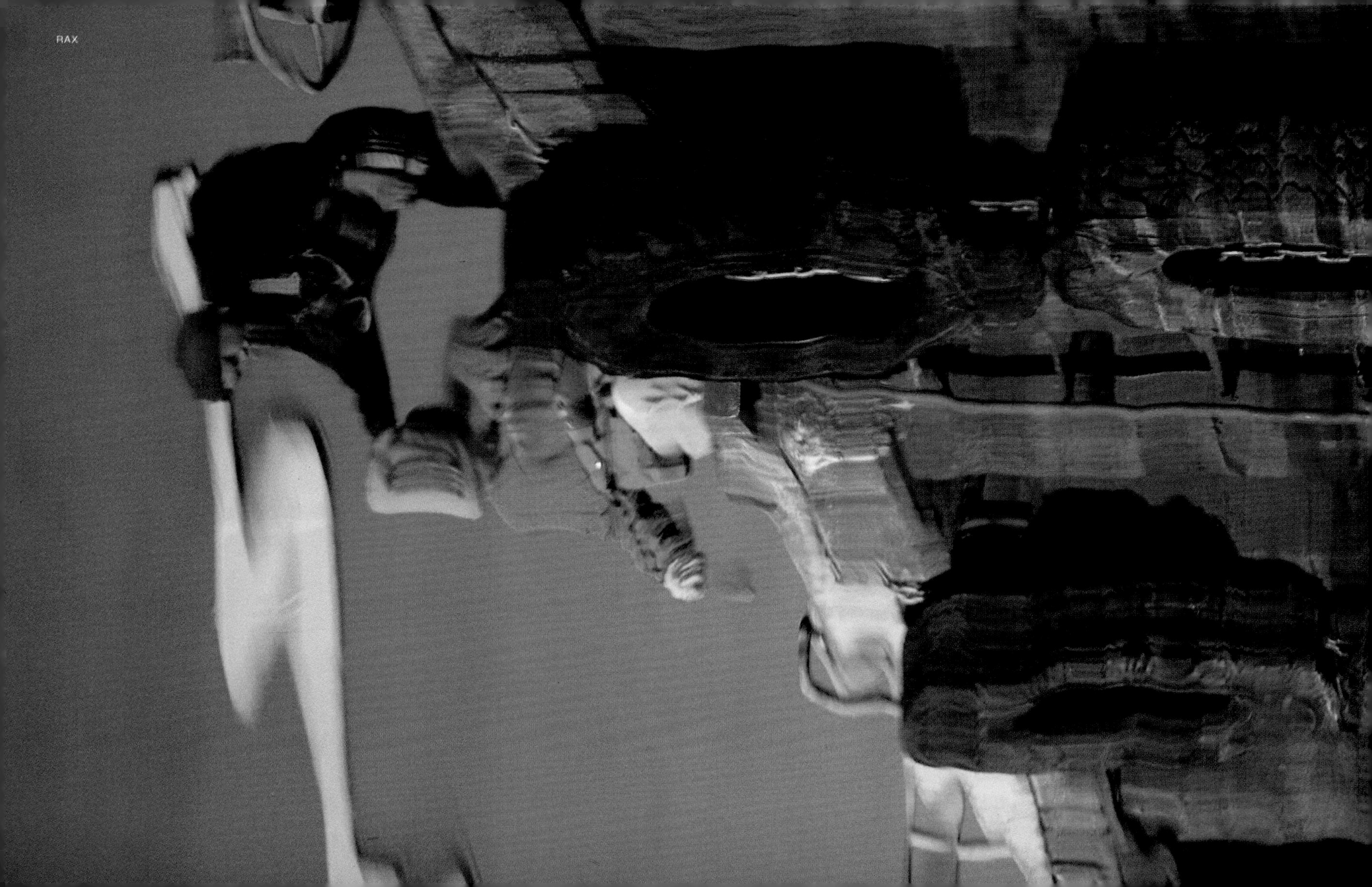

RAX

MUSSELS WITH LEMON SAUCE

20-30 mussels
seasoned stock:
1 onion
5 black peppercorn
1/2 tsp salt
1 bay leaf
2 stalks parsley
1 carrot, chopped
1.5 l (2 5/8 pt 6 1/2 cup) water
1 dl (3 1/2 fl oz 1/2 cup) white wine
1/4 dl (1 fl oz 1/8 cup) white wine vinegar
1 dl (3 1/2 fl oz 1/2 cup) fish stock

Sauce:
1 lemon
1/2 onion
1 dl (3 1/2 fl oz 1/2 cup) white wine
2 dl (7 fl oz 7/8 cup) cream
salt
pepper
150 g (5 oz) butter

Wash and trim the mussels. Put the water in a large pot. Add the seasoned stock. Bring to the boil with the lid on. Simmer while making the sauce. When the sauce is ready boil the mussels rapidly in the stock.

Sauce:

Chop the onion and fry until soft in 20 g of butter and a pinch of salt. Add the white wine and reduce by half by simmering. Pour in the cream, simmer for a few minutes. Cut the cold butter into pieces and add to the cream. Stir vigorously but do not boil. Spoon the sauce over the mussels. Serve with bread and salad. Note that the strained broth may be frozen for later use.

Iceland's glaciers are a world of their own, where bottomless crevasses alternate with bizarre ice sculptures, and ancient volcanic craters thrust up through the ice. Iceland's largest glacier, Vatnajökull, is also the largest in Europe.

SEAFOOD BAG WITH SHELLFISH

4 fillo pastry sheets
2 tbsp oil
1 tbsp butter
1/2 onion
2 mushrooms
1/2 red bell pepper
1 clove garlic
1 tsp chopped parsley
1 tsp chopped tarragon
4 lobster tails (cut in two and shell removed)
8 scallops
10 shelled shrimps
6 mussels
Sauce:
4 tomatoes
2 tsp chives
1/2 onion
1/4 dl (1 fl oz 1/8 cup) white wine
salt
pepper
juice of shellfish
1 tbsp oil

To make the sauce: Place the tomatoes in boiling water for a few seconds and then straight into iced water. Remove the skin. Mix the tomatoes in a mixer. Chop the onion and fry until soft. Add a dash of pepper and salt and pour in the wine. Simmer down by half. Pour in the tomatoes and add the chives. Simmer slowly for 35-40 minutes. Prefry scallops, lobster, shrimps and mussels in oil for twenty seconds and mix into a bowl. Chop onion, mushrooms, peppers, the garlic, parsley and tarragon and fry all in butter in a pan. Pour the mixture over the fish and mix carefully. Place in a sieve and use the juice thus obtained for the tomato sauce. Heat the oven to 200°C (400°F). Arrange the mixture centrally on two layers of pastry sheets and contract them into a bag. Place on a baking sheet and fry until the bag has turned golden brown.

STEAMED HADDOCK FILLETS

400 g (14 oz) fillets of haddock
2 sheets of grease-proof paper
50 g (2 oz) butter
salt
pepper
1 clove garlic
1 sprig parsley
4 mushrooms
1/2 leek
2 carrots
6 mangetout beans
2 shallots

Wash the vegetables. Cut the carrots rather finely and the mushrooms in four. Chop coarsely leek, parsley, beans, shallots and garlic. Cut the haddock in pieces. Cut large circles from the paper and cover with the butter. Place the fish on the grease-proof paper and season with pepper and salt. Place the vegetables over the fish and around it and cover tightly. Bake on a grill or in an oven for about 5-7 minutes.

TROUT FILLETS WITH CHEESE AND ALMONDS

400 g (14 oz) trout fillets
100 g (3 1/2 oz) camembert cheese
30 g (1 oz) almond flakes
1/2 dl (2 fl oz 1/4 cup) cream
salt
1 tsp caster sugar
oil for frying

Gently purée the camembert cheese in a mixer together with the almonds and the caster sugar. Add the cream and stir together. Fry the fillets and season with a pinch of salt. Place the fish on a baking sheet. Spread the purée on it. Place under the grill in the oven for about 2-3 minutes or until the cheese is golden brown. Serve with vegetables of your choice.

SKATE WITH NUTS AND BLUE CHEESE

2-4 fresh skate wings (depending on size)
oil for frying
100 g (3 1/2 oz) butter

Sauce:
60 g (2 oz) blue cheese
30 g (1 oz) cashew nuts
10 g (1/3 oz) butter
1 onion
1 dl (3 1/2 fl oz 1/2 cup) red wine
1 dl (3 1/2 fl oz 1/2 cup) beef stock
salt
pepper

Roll the wings in flour and cut a diamond pattern into the flesh. Season with salt and pepper. Fry in oil until nicely brown. Place in the oven with pieces of butter on top at 170°C (340°F).

To prepare the sauce: Brown the nuts in butter, add the chopped onion and fry until soft. Then pour in the red wine. Reduce by half by simmering. Add the cheese and finally the thick beef stock. Season with salt and pepper to taste. Arrange the wings on a plate and pour sauce over them. Serve with vegetables of your choice.

The Snæfellsjökull glacier is reputed to possess mystic and supernatural powers. Magical or not, the glacier is a memorable sight as the Midnight Sun blurs the edges of day and night into a long sunset-sunrise, and the icecap floats eerily on the horizon.

RAX

Reykjavík in winter. Snow veils the city, and kids rush out to play, with their skis and sledges.

RAX

FRIED COD TONGUES (GELLUR) WITH CURRY AND COCONUT

Gellur, tasty tongue muscles and a very popular dish in Iceland, can be cooked and served in various ways.

400 g (14 oz) cod tongues
2 eggs
2 tbsp shredded coconut
1 sprig finely chopped dill
1 red apple
1/2 pineapple
1 carrot
1 red onion
salt
pepper
2 tbsp curry powder
1 dl (3 1/2 fl oz 1/2 cup) white wine
2 dl (7 fl oz 7/8 cup) cream
cornflour
oil for frying
50 g (2 oz) butter

Beat the eggs and mix them with the coconut and the chopped dill. Season the cod tongues with salt and pepper. Roll the cod tongues in flour and place them in the egg mixture. Cut the carrot, onion, apple and pineapple into small cubes. Melt butter in a pot and add the curry. Stir carefully while adding the fruit and vegetables. Pour the white wine into the pot and simmer for 2-3 minutes. Finally, add the cream and let the sauce simmer at a low temperature for two minutes. Thicken with cornflour. Add salt and pepper. Fry cod tongues in oil in a deep pan to a golden colour. Arrange the curry mixture on a plate and place the cod tongues on top of it. Serve with rice.

GLAZED SALMON

400 g (14 oz) salmon fillets
2 eggs
20 g caster sugar
1 tsp mild curry
1 dl (3 1/2 fl oz 1/2 cup) white wine
4 pasta sheets
salt
pepper

Cut the salmon into thin slices. Boil the pasta sheets and dry. Break the eggs into a bowl. Mix the caster sugar, the white wine and the curry. Place the bowl in warm water and whip together until well thickened (a balloon whisk is preferable), remove. Continue beating the sauce to cool it.

Start the grill of the oven. Note that heatproof plates or moulds have to be used. Place one pasta sheet on a plate. Dry the salmon carefully and season with salt and pepper. Arrange the slices on the pasta, spread a little of the curry cream on the salmon and put the other pasta sheet on top and spread the cream on the pasta. Glaze the salmon under the grill for 4-6 minutes. Serve.

Icelanders have been fishing for salmon since the Middle Ages. In olden times, salmon was caught in nets laid in the rivers, but today the approach is more sportsmanlike. Iceland boasts some of the best salmon rivers in Europe.

Lamb

For more than a thousand years the sheep was one of the mainstays of farming.

Innumerable stories of shepherds looking for sheep in mountains and highlands and frequently meeting elves, highland fugitives or ghosts have been handed down from generation to generation.

Many stories are related of men who while looking for sheep met elves who invited them to their homes. There were even instances of men who married beautiful elfish maidens and went to live with them in elfland. The farming, agriculture and historical heritage of the nation are thus intertwined. In our times lamb is extremely popular in the Saga Island and the preparation of it has radically changed in the past few decades. It may be asserted that in this period the Icelanders discovered the enormous culinary possibilities of lamb and these possibilities are far from being exhausted. The Icelandic sheep is known for many matchless merits. For centuries sheep have been nourished by the vegetation of the highlands. The Icelandic sheep stock has remained pure and has adapted to Icelandic conditions. Even in winter sheep are known to be put out to graze where the snow is not too deep. The most natural lamb in the world, s´il vous plait!

RAX

Ice-floes break off from a tongue of the Vatnajökull glacier, to drift on the waters of the Jökulsárlón lagoon. The temperature of the water is close to freezing point. This unique spectacle is a popular tourist destination.

LAMB FILLET WITH CAPERS AND TOMATOES

360 g (13 oz) fillet of lamb
4 tomatoes
2 shallots
3 tbsp parsley
1 tsp sage
1/2 dl (2 fl oz 1/4 cup) white wine
4 tbsp capers
1 yellow bell pepper
1/2 zucchini
salt
pepper
oil

Peel and purée the tomatoes in a mixer. Finely chop the shallots, parsley and sage and fry lightly in butter. Pour in the white wine and reduce just a little. Put the tomato purée in the pot. Simmer for about 10-12 minutes at a low heat. Meantime, cut bell pepper and zucchini to matchstick size and add them with the capers to the tomatoes. Cut the fillets into rather small pieces and fry rapidly, seasoning with salt and pepper. Put the tomato purée on a plate and the lamb on top. Serve with fried potato slices.

LEG OF LAMB WITH GAME SAUCE

360 g (13 oz) boned leg of lamb
30 g (1 oz) wild mushrooms
10 g (1/3 oz) mushrooms
1 tsp rosemary
1 tsp sage
30 g (1 oz) blue cheese
2 tsp jam
1 dl (3 1/2 fl oz 1/2 cup) beef stock
1 dl (3 1/2 fl oz 1/2 cup) cream
2 tbsp bitters (jaegermeister)
salt
pepper

Brown the lamb. Season with salt and pepper, remove. Heat the oven to 180°C (350°F). Fry the mushrooms and season with the herbs. Add the jam, then the cream, blue cheese, game stock and finally the bitters. Place meat in the oven for 3-4 minutes. Put sauce on the plate and slices of lamb on it. Serve with vegetables and potatoes to taste.

PÁLL

To the Icelanders, the bellshaped flowers of the campanula signify youth and innocence. Floral splendour in the Skaftafell National Park.

The Icelandic horse has adapted to the difficult conditions of the Icelandic winter, growing a thick winter "overcoat" to keep him warm in the chilliest of weather. When he sheds his heavy coat in summer, he can be groomed to shining perfection.

LAMB CHOPS EN CROUTE WITH STRAWBERRRY SAUCE

8 lamb chops with rib
2 sheets fillo pastry
4 mushrooms
40 g (1 1/2 oz) ham
2 small red onions
bread crumbs
2 leaves mint, fresh
8 fresh strawberries
1/2 dl (2 fl oz 1/4 cup) port wine
1/2 dl (2 fl oz 1/4 cup) beef stock, thickened
1/2 dl (2 fl oz 1/4 cup) cream
1 tbsp butter
sage
salt
pepper

Cut the ham, 1 onion and mushrooms into pieces. Fry in the oil. Season with mint leaves sage, salt and pepper. Purée in a mixer, sprinkle with bread crumbs (to dry the mixture) and place aside. Trim the chops, scrape the bones and cut away all fat. Season with mint leaves, sage, salt and pepper. Brown the chops in hot oil. Remove. Spread the chops with the purée. Cut the fillo sheets in four and wrap them round each chop. Heat the oven to 230°C (450°F). Chop the other red onion finely and tenderize in the butter. Pour in the port wine and reduce by half. Take half of the strawberries and cut them into the port wine. Add beef stock and finally the cream. Boil just a little and season with salt and pepper. Meanwhile, fry the chops in the oven for 7-8 minutes. Cut the remaining strawberries in slices and arrange them on the plate, the sauce on top of them and finally the chops.

RAX

Basaltic rock, eroded by alternating heat and cold. Water collects and freezes, forming cracks and hollows in the solid rock.

PALL

LAMB ROLL WITH PRUNES AND DATES

i0 g (13 oz) lamb fillet
cup cous-cous
cup water
tomatoes
) pitted dates
pitted prunes
yellow bell pepper
2 aubergine
tbsp olive oil
2 head iceberg lettuce
hite wine vinegar
lt
pper

Chop prunes and dates. Cut the lamb fillet sideways but not right through. Unfold. Season with salt and pepper, put prunes and dates on the fillet. Roll up in a plastic film and tie the ends. Boil at low heat for 7-8 minutes. Boil cous cous in water, strain and cool. Cut vegetables and sautée in olive oil except the iceberg and tomatoes. Mix all with the cous-cous. Arrange on a plate. Combine in a bowl chopped parsley, 1 tbsp white wine vinegar and 2 tbsp olive oil. Sprinkle over vegetables. Remove lamb from plastic film, cut in slices and serve with vegetables.

SADDLE OF LAMB WITH MUSTARD

800 g (1 lb 12 oz) saddle of lamb (rib side)
50 g (2 oz) mushrooms
1 tbsp rose pepper
2 shallots
1/2 tsp basil
1/2 tsp oregano
1/2 tsp thyme
1/4 tsp rosemary
1 tbsp parsley
1 dl (3 1/2 fl oz 1/2 cup) lamb stock
1 dl (3 1/2 fl oz 1/2 cup) rosé wine
2 tbsp dijon mustard
100 g (3 1/2 oz) butter
salt
pepper
2 tbsp garlic oil

Chop the mushrooms, shallots and herbs. Fry in the garlic oil and brown well. Add the rose pepper. Pour in the rosé wine and reduce by 1/3. Now add the lamb stock and thicken with some cornflour. Simmer while preparing the lamb. Cut the fat from the ribs. Trim the meat. Cut a diamond pattern in the fat on the meat and season with salt and pepper. Heat the oven to 200°C (400°F). Roast until top is golden brown. Cover with a thin layer of mustard and roast in the oven for 10 minutes. Turn off the heat and leave for 5 minutes. Add butter to the sauce. Serve with potato gratin.

Iceland offers many opportunities for leisure activities in unspoilt natural surroundings. The Icelandic horse, once the Icelanders' only form of transport, is the ideal travelling companion.

FILLET OF LAMB WITH OLIVES

360 g (13 oz) lamb fillet
1/2 dl (2 fl oz 1/4 cup) lamb stock
1 dl (3 1/2 fl oz 1/2 cup) red wine
2 tbsp crôutons
100 g (3 1/2 oz) butter
8 tiny onions
2 tbsp pistachios
10 black olives
4 cloves of garlic
a dash of red wine vinegar
salt
pepper
oil for frying

Heat the oven to 180°C (350°F). Sautée the olives, nuts, onion and garlic in a pan together with the lamb. Brown the lamb for 1/2 minute each side, and turn vegetables frequently in the pan and dash with red wine vinegar. Transfer the lamb from the pan into the oven. Pour the red wine into the pan and reduce by 1/3. Add cold pieces of butter with 1/2 dl of the lamb stock. Place the meat on a plate and the vegetables over it. Sprinkle with the crôutons.

Mountains, lake and snow combine to create a spectacular panorama at the aptly-named Veiðivötn (Fishing Lakes), which teem with fish.

PÁLL

Arnarstapi, unapproachable by humans, is only for the birds - even its name is a reminder of the eagle, the king of Icelandic birds.

ODDUR

LAMB SHANK WITH ROSE PEPPER

2 shanks of lamb
4 shallots
4 tbsp rose pepper
0.3 dl (0.8 fl oz) cognac
2 dl (7 fl oz 7/8 cup) lamb stock
salt
pepper
100 g (3 1/2 oz) butter
1 dl (3 1/2 fl oz 1/2 cup) water
oil

Brown the shanks of lamb in a pan and season with salt and pepper. Then place them in an oven pan at 170°C (340°F) for about 70-80 minutes. After 40 minutes put 50 g of clarified butter and 1 dl of water in the oven tray and baste the meat with this every now and then. Chop the shallots finely and fry until soft. Then add the rose pepper without browning. Pour in the cognac and then the lamb stock. Simmer for 3-4 minutes. Finally season with salt and pepper and add butter. Pour sauce over the meat and serve with vegetables to taste.

FILLET OF LAMB WITH MUSHROOMS

360 g (13 oz) fillet of lamb
80 g (2 1/2 oz) assorted wild mushrooms
20 g (2/3 oz) mushrooms
1 dl (3 1/2 fl oz 1/2 cup) beef stock
1/2 dl (2 fl oz 1/4 cup) Madeira (port wine)
100 g (3 1/2 oz) butter
corn flour
oil for frying
salt
pepper

Heat the oven to 180°C (350°F). Cut the mushrooms into thick slices. Heat a pan with 1 tbsp of oil. Brown the lamb and season with salt and pepper. Set aside. Fry mushrooms for 2-3 minutes in 50 g of butter in a pan. Pour the Madeira into the pan and reduce by half by simmering. Add the beef stock and boil for about 2 minutes more. Thicken with cornflour. Add cold butter to it. Place meat in the oven for 3 minutes, turn off the oven and keep there for another 3 minutes. Arrange the mushrooms on a plate and put the meat on top. Pour the sauce over meat. Vegetables to taste.

RAX

ROAST LEG OF LAMB WITH HERBS

1 leg of lamb
1 dl oil for cooking
1 tbsp chopped parsley
1 tsp chopped oregano
1 tsp chopped thyme
1/4 tsp chopped rosemary
1 tsp chopped mint
1 tsp chopped basil
1 tbsp crushed rose pepper
4 crushed cloves of garlic
1 tsp crushed black peppercorns
salt

Trim the leg of lamb and cut away all excess fat. Season with salt. Set the oven at 220°C (425°F). Mix the chopped herbs, pepper and garlic with the oil. Blend thoroughly. Cover the leg thoroughly with the mixture. Roast the leg on a rack with an oven tray under it for about 30 minutes and turn off the oven. Leave in the oven for another 30 minutes. Serve with baked potatoes, garlic and onions.

Dyrhólaey stands out where the north Atlantic waves pound Iceland's southern coast. Vessels can sail through the hole in the rock, gouged by furious seas.

ROAST LAMB EN CROUTE

360 g (13 oz) leg of lamb, boned
4 fillo pastry sheets
60 g (2 oz) blue cheese
2 tsp redcurrant jam
oil for cooking
1/2 onion
1 dl (3 1/2 fl oz 1/2 cup) lamb stock, thickened with cornflour
1 dl (3 1/2 fl oz 1/2 cup) port wine
8 green grapes, stoned
100 g (3 1/2 oz) butter
salt
pepper

Brown the meat in a pan. Spread half of the blue cheese in a thin layer on the meat after drying it carefully. Then add the jam. Form a bag of the pastry round the meat. Heat the oven to 200°C (400°F). Chop the onion finely and fry until soft. Pour in the port wine. Reduce by half by simmering. Pour in the lamb stock together with the rest of the cheese and season with salt and pepper to taste. Place the lamb in the oven for 10 minutes. Turn it off and leave for 3 minutes. Meanwhile, add cold pieces of butter to the sauce and finally the grapes. Serve with vegetables to taste. Pour the sauce on the plate and place the meat on top of it.

Although Icelanders are originally a fishing and farming community there is no long hunting tradition in this country comparable with the continent of Europe. Reindeer, ptarmigans, ducks and geese are the most common and popular kinds of wild game. Reindeer were not among the original fauna of Iceland but were imported in 1771 from Lapland. The purpose was to exploit the animals, both their meat and skins, as the Lapps do. The animals live in large herds in the eastern highlands of Iceland and are hunted by sportsmen in the wild. The three species of fowl, ptarmigan, duck and goose, enjoy enormous popularity. The ptarmigan is caught in early winter until Christmas and is a traditional Christmas dish in many homes. The custom of shooting wild geese and ducks is more recent. Iceland boasts the largest breeding population of geese in Europe. Icelandic wild game is renowned for its consistently delicious taste. The mild flavour of the moorland herbs which might be called the spice of nature is absorbed into the meat to make it incomparable.

Wild Game

PÁLL

PÁLL

PTARMIGAN WITH RASPBERRY SAUCE

2 ptarmigans, skinned and trimmed
20 raspberries
1/2 dl (2 fl oz 1/4 cup) port wine
1/2 dl (2 fl oz 1/4 cup) cream
1 dl (3 fl oz 1/2 cup) game stock
2 tbsp lemon melissa
2 shallots
salt
pepper
oil

Lightly fry the ptarmigans in a pan. Remove and place in oven tray and season with salt and pepper. Heat oven to 180°C (350°F). Thicken the game stock. Chop shallots and lemon melissa and heat in 1 tbsp oil on the pan. Add port wine and 15 raspberries. Simmer for 5 minutes. Add game stock and finally the cream. Simmer for 2-3 minutes. Place ptarmigan in oven for 5-6 minutes, turn off the heat and leave for 4-5 minutes. Serve with sauce and vegetables to taste. Garnish with the rest of the raspberries.

REINDEER ROAST WITH WILD MUSHROOMS

360 g (13 oz) reindeer fillet
2 shallots
50 g (2 oz) wild mushrooms
3 tbsp chopped thyme
1 tbsp blackcurrant jam
1/2 dl (2 fl oz 1/4 cup) Madeira (port wine)
1/4 dl (1 fl oz 1/8 cup) cream
1/4 dl (1 fl oz 1/8 cup) malt beer
salt
pepper
oil for frying

Season the reindeer fillet. Heat the oven to 170°C (325°F). Chop shallots. Slice mushrooms. Fry the fillet on both sides. Remove and place in oven tray. Sautée onion, thyme and mushrooms in 1 tbsp of oil for 2 minutes. Pour the wine in the pan and reduce by half; then add blackcurrant jam, cream and malt beer. Place reindeer fillet in oven for 5 minutes, turn off heat and keep for 3 minutes. Put the meat for a short while in the sauce. Can be served with bell pepper, mushrooms and sautéed potatoes.

At Látrabjarg, one of Iceland's most spectacular spots, millions of seabirds nest on rocky ledges. Eggs were traditionally collected from the sheer cliff face, by swinging down the rock on ropes. The practice continues today, although on a much smaller scale.

ODDUR

WILD GOOSE BREAST

2 goose breasts
50 g (2 oz) blue cheese
1 tsp red currant jam
4 mushrooms
2 shallots
1 dl (3 1/2 fl oz 1/2 cup) cream
1 dl (3 1/2 fl oz 1/2 cup) game stock
1/4 dl (1 fl oz 1/8 cup) sherry
salt
pepper
oil

Heat the oven to 170°C (325°F). Fry the goose breasts on both sides, season with salt and pepper. Place in the oven tray. Thicken the stock with cornflour, simmer for a while. Finely chop the onion. Cut the mushrooms and sautée with onions in oil. Pour in the sherry followed by blue cheese and jam. Put the goose breasts in the oven. Roast for 5 minutes. Turn off the oven and keep for another 5 minutes. Finally add the cream to the sauce. Serve.

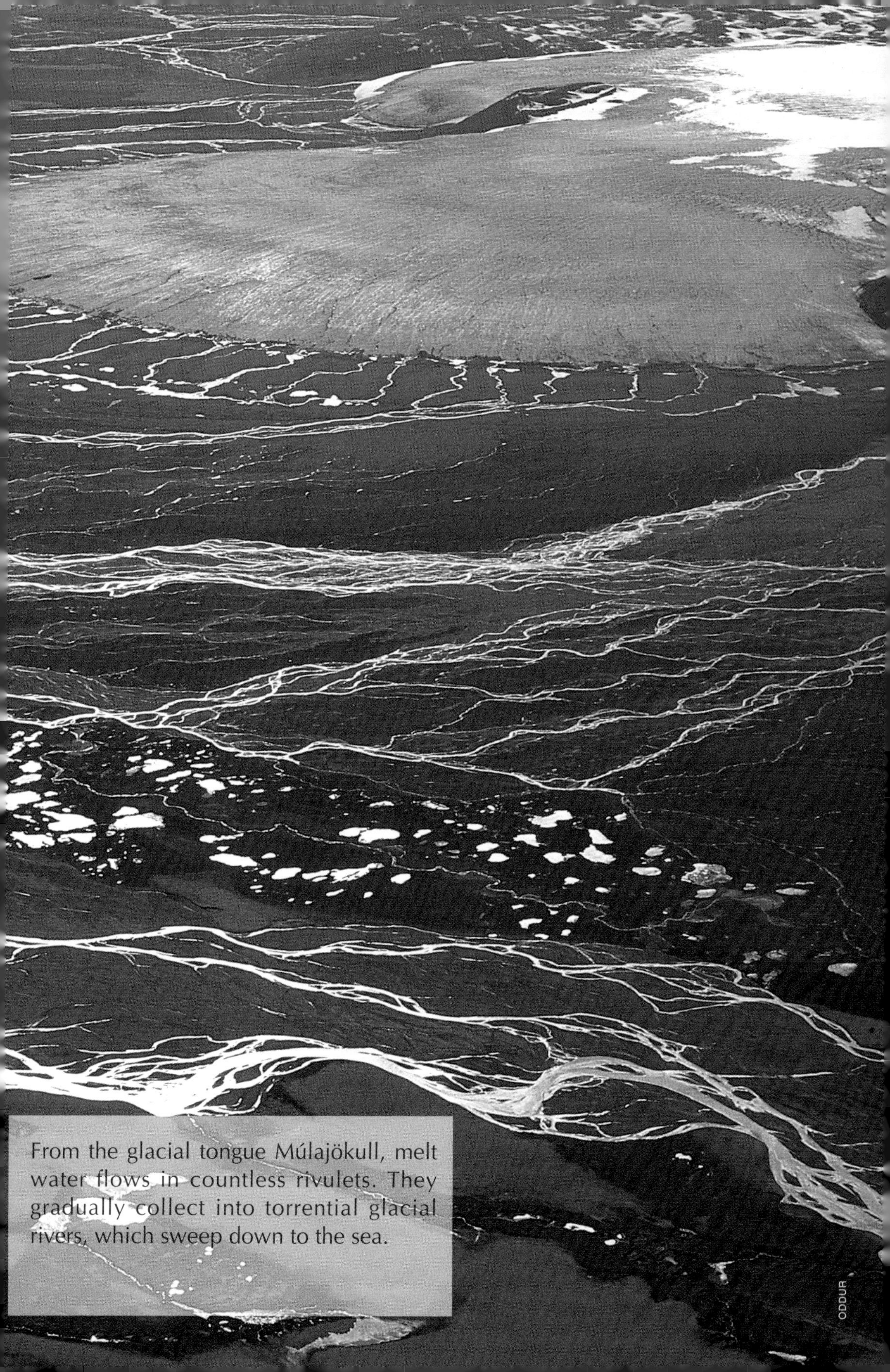

From the glacial tongue Múlajökull, melt water flows in countless rivulets. They gradually collect into torrential glacial rivers, which sweep down to the sea.

BREAST OF DUCK WITH DATES

2 wild duck breasts
2 plums
10 dates
1 dl (3 1/2 fl oz 1/2 cup) wild duck stock
1/2 dl (2 fl oz 1/4 cup) plum liqueur
salt
pepper
2 tbsp honey
80 g (2 1/2 oz) butter

Trim the duck breasts. Cut dates and plums in small pieces. Thicken game stock. Fry breasts until golden brown and spread with honey. Place in oven tray. Heat oven to 170°C (325°F). Put half the plums and all the dates into a pot. Pour in the liqueur and simmer for about 1 minute. Add game stock and reduce by 1/3. Put in the rest of the plums. Roast duck in oven for about 4 minutes, turn off oven and keep for 5 minutes more. Put butter in the sauce and stir gently. Place the duck on a plate and pour sauce over it.

Desserts

CHOCOLATE ICE CREAM CAKE

5 egg yolks
1 egg
5 tbsp caster sugar
1/2 litre (18 fl oz 2 1/4 cup) cream
1/2 dl (2 fl oz 1/4 cup) Kahlua liqueur
1 dl (3 fl oz 1/2 cup) chocolate sauce
4 tbsp shredded chocolate
10 oat biscuits
6 chocolate biscuits
130 g (4 1/2 oz) butter
1 cake mould

Melt butter. Crush oat biscuits and chocolate biscuits and mix with butter. Press into mould, cool. Whip the egg yolks and egg with the caster sugar to a fluffy mixture. Whip the cream. Gently mix the chocolate sauce, Kahlua and crushed chocolate with the eggs, and then the cream. Pour into mould. Put into the freezer and keep it there for at least 6 hours. Serve with chocolate sauce and whipped cream.

Ljótipollur does not live up to its discouraging name (Ugly Pond). The tired traveller can see his reflection in the still blue waters of the "ugly pond," while he discerns troll-like images in the shadowy slopes.

PÁLL

Thymus praecox, a variety of thyme, is a well-known Icelandic herbal remedy, still used today to ease various ills. Like other favourite Icelandic plants, it adds a welcome touch of colour to the brief northern summer.

ODDUR

RASPBERRY CHEESE CAKE

400 g (14 oz) cream cheese
150 g (5 oz) caster sugar
3 dl (1/2 pt 1 1/4 cup) cream
100 g (3 1/2 oz) raspberries
50 g (2 oz) blackberries
6 gelatine sheets
1 dl (3 1/2 fl oz 1/2 cup) raspberry juice
100 g (3 1/2 oz) salted peanuts
15 oat biscuits
130 g (4 1/2 oz) butter
cake mould

Melt butter. Crush peanuts and oat biscuits. Pour in butter and mix well. Press into cake mould and cool. Whip cream cheese and caster sugar together and 2/3 of the berries. Whip the cream slightly. Melt gelatine in the raspberry juice. Add cream cheese to cream and finally the raspberry juice with gelatine (the juice must have cooled to lukewarm before being added to the mixture). Place in the mould and cool for at least 4 hours. Serve with the rest of the berries.

BLUEBERRY SKYR CAKE

400 g (14 oz) skyr
2.5 dl (9 fl oz 1 1/8 cup) cream
6 gelatine sheets
100 g (3 1/2 oz) blueberries
180 g (6 oz) caster sugar
2 tbsp blueberry jam
12 oat biscuits
120 g (4 1/2 oz) butter
1 cake mould

Melt butter. Finely crush oat biscuits. Add the melted butter. Press together into mould and cool. Melt gelatine sheets in bain marie. Stir skyr with caster sugar and 80 g of blueberries. Whip cream. Gently stir skyr mixture with cream and finally add gelatine. Spread blueberry jam on the bottom. Pour skyr mixture into mould. Keep in a fridge for at least 6 hours. Serve with whipped cream and blueberry sauce. Curd cheese can be substituted for skyr.

Traditional Dishes

The Icelandic culinary tradition is best represented by the good old home cooking. For some Icelanders, especially of the older generation, the only real food is well prepared home cooking. Many of them would prefer saltmeat and peas to elaborate dishes, garnished a la mode. This is not strange considering that home cooking, prepared from first-class raw material, is deeply rooted in the national mentality. Every Icelander knows exactly what is meant by home cooking. Icelandic home cooking is classic and has changed little over the centuries, remaining both traditional and everyday. And if we are going to follow a true Icelandic culinary tradition we will have a coffee with fruitcake or pancake after the main dish, which is still widely the custom in the rural parts of the country.

RAX

ROAST LEG OF LAMB
(ofnbakað lambalæri)

450 g (1 lb) leg of lamb
1 tbsp melted butter
1 1/2 tbsp salt
1 tsp crushed black pepper
3 dl (1/2 pt 1 1/4 cup) water or lamb stock
30 g (1 oz) butter
30 g (1 oz) flour
1 tsp chopped onion

Remove all excess fat. Mix butter, salt and pepper and season the leg. Place the leg on a rack over oven tray. Fry at 180°C (350°F) for 40 minutes. Reduce heat to approximately 80-100°C (200°F). Pour lamb stock or water into oven tray and leave for another 20 minutes. Remove tray from oven and scraps from the bottom. Pour through muslin in a sieve to avoid the fat.

Thicken stock with a mixture of flour and butter. Cream may be added to sauce. Season with salt and pepper if necessary. Add gravy browning if preferred. For the last 5 minutes the leg is kept under the oven grill to obtain a nice brown colour. Serve with caramelised potatoes, green peas, red cabbage and rhubarb jam.

ROASTED SADDLE OF LAMB
(ofnbakaður lambahryggur)

450 (1 lb) saddle of lamb
2 tbsp oil
1 1/2 tsp salt
1 tsp freshly ground pepper
3 dl (1/2 pt) (1 1/4 cup) lamb stock or water
30 g (1 oz) butter
30 g (1 oz) flour

Mix together salt and pepper in oil and rub into the meat. Set oven at 160°C (315°F), place the saddle on a rack in the oven with a tray underneath it. Roast for 1 hour and 20 minutes. Pour 3 dl of lamb stock or water into oven tray after 30 minutes. Remove tray from oven when 15 minutes are left and strain the stock through a muslin cloth in a sieve. Thicken stock with the flour and butter. Add salt and pepper. Cream may also be added as well as gravy browning. Serve with red cabbage, green peas, caramelised potatoes and rhubarb jam.

STEWED FISH
(plokkfiskur)

300 g (11 oz) fish
3 tbsp chopped onion
2 dl (7 fl oz 7/8 cup) milk
1 dl (3 1/2 fl oz 1/2 cup) cream
40 g (1 1/3 oz) flour
40 g (1 1/3 oz) butter
100 g (3 1/2 oz) boiled potatoes
salt
pepper

Boil fish in lightly salted water. Remove from water when done. Melt butter in a pot, add the flour and stir. Pour in cream and milk and stir well until mixture is well thickened. Add onion and potatoes cut in pieces. Season with salt and pepper. Finally add fish and mix everything thoroughly. Serve with rye bread.

BOILED SALTFISH
(soðinn saltfiskur)

400 g (12 1/2 oz) saltfish
water

Boil the saltfish at a low heat for 8-10 minutes depending on the size of the pieces. Serve with butter or suet, potatoes and vegetables of your own choice.

BOILED HADDOCK

(soðin ýsa)

400 g (14 oz) haddock
water
salt
2 black peppercorns
1/2 bay leaf

The fish used to be cut in large slices and boiled in water. Nowadays it is often filleted and boiled at a low heat for just a few minutes to retain its vitamins and natural juices. This cooked fish is still served with melted butter as well as potatoes and vegetables.

FISHBALLS

(fiskibollur)

300 g (11 oz) fish mince (cod or haddock)
60 g (2 oz) flour
2 dl (7 fl oz 7/8 cup) milk
1 egg
1 onion
salt
pepper
butter

Mix the dry ingredients. Whip together milk and egg. Chop onion. Mix beaten eggs and dry ingredients alternately with fish mince. Finally add onion. Keep covered in a fridge for about 1 hour. Melt butter in a pan. Form oblong balls using two spoons. Fry balls in butter. Place in an oven tray and simmer for a few minutes. Serve with potatoes, butter and sautéed onions.

FRIED HADDOCK IN BREAD CRUMBS (steikt ýsa í raspi)

400 g (14 oz) haddock
1 egg
1 dl (3 1/2 fl oz 1/2 cup) milk
2 tbsp flour
salt
pepper
2 tbsp butter
bread crumbs

Cut fish in pieces. Season with salt and pepper. Toss in flour. Mix together egg and milk and put the fish in mixture, cover with bread crumbs. Fry fish in oil and butter on each side for 1-2 minutes. Serve with potatoes and butter, even onion butter.

DEEPFRIED FISH IN PASTRY (djúpsteiktur fiskur)

400 g (14 oz) cod or haddock
250 g (9 oz) flour
2 dl (7 fl oz 7/8 cup) beer
1 egg
1 tsp salt
1/4 tsp pepper
1 tsp sugar
1/2 tsp paprika powder
1/2 dl (2 fl oz 1/4 cup) oil

Mix the dry ingredients. Add beer to the flour and then the egg. Keep in a fridge for about 1/2 hour. Cut fish into serving size. Toss in flour. Dip pieces in batter. Deepfry for 3-4 minutes. Serve with fresh salad and even french fries.

BOILED LEG OF SMOKED LAMB *(soðið hangikjöt)*

450 g (1 lb) smoked leg of lamb
1 l (1 3/4 pt 4 1/2 cups) water
1 tbsp sugar
3 dl (1/2 pt 1 1/4 cup) milk
1/2 dl (2 fl oz 1/4 cup) cream

Place the leg in an oven tray, add the sweetened water and cover with foil. Set the oven at 160°C (315°F). Boil for about 2 hours. Serve with boiled potatoes in Béchamel milk sauce. Also serve with red cabbage, green peas, and carrots.

FRIED MEAT BALLS *(steiktar kjötbollur)*

300 g (11 oz) lamb
1/2 onion
1 tbsp cornflour
1/2 dl (2 fl oz 1/4 cup) milk
1/2 dl (2 fl oz 1/4 cup) water
1 egg
salt
pepper
2 onions
2 1/2 dl (9 fl oz 1 1/8 cup) lamb stock or water
2 tbsp butter

Mince 1/2 onion and meat. Add flour, egg, water and milk. Season with salt and pepper. Cool for 1/2 hour. Shape oblong balls from the dough and fry in a pan for about 6 minutes. Pour lamb stock into the pan and thicken. Cut 2 onions in slices and fry in butter. Serve meat balls with sauce, onions, potatoes and vegetables.

LAMB CHOPS
(kótelettur í raspi)

10 lamb chops
2 dl (7 fl oz 7/8 cup) milk
1 egg
100 g (3 1/2 oz) bread crumbs
100 g (3 1/2 oz) flour
salt
pepper
butter and oil for frying

Season the chops with salt and pepper. Toss in flour. Dip into mixture of milk and egg, then in the bread crumbs, with the chops well covered. Fry in butter and oil in a pan for 1-2 minutes each side. Reduce heat under pan, cover with lid and simmer for 5-6 minutes more or place in oven tray at 170°C (325°F) for a few minutes. Serve with butter, potatoes boiled or caramelised, red cabbage and green peas.

MINCED MEAT WITH ONION
(hakkað buff með lauk)

180 g (6 oz) minced lamb
2 onions
2 tbsp butter
oil
salt
pepper
flour
2 eggs

Shape meat into flat patties and season with salt and pepper. Chop onions. Fry the meat and onions in the pan in oil. Turn the meat and add the butter. Reduce heat. Fry the eggs. Serve with boiled potatoes and pickles.

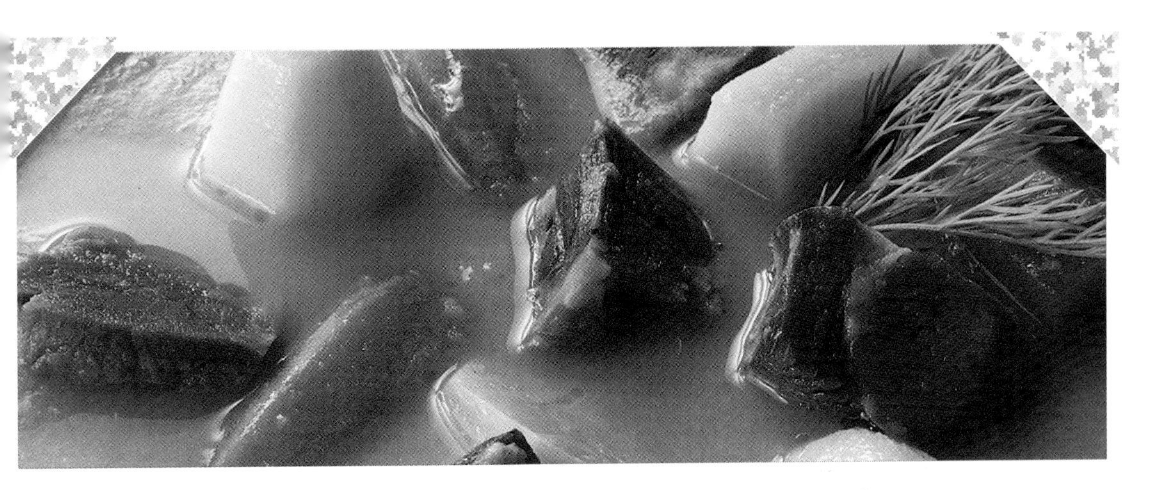

SALT MEAT AND YELLOW PEA SOUP *(saltkjöt og baunir)*

400 g (14 oz) salt lamb
50 g (2 oz) yellow split peas
6 dl (1 pt 2 5/8 cup) water
1 onion
4 potatoes
200 g (7 oz) carrots
200 g (7 oz) swedes/rutabaga
1 tsp thyme

Soak split peas in water for a few hours. Peel onions and cut in pieces. Sieve the water from the peas and put in a pot with onions and 6 dl water. Boil at moderate heat for an hour and a half. Put one piece of meat with peeled swedes, potatoes and carrots (all cut in pieces) into the pot. Add thyme. Boil for 20 minutes. Boil the rest of the meat in water for one to 1 1/4 hours. Serve in a bowl of soup or with the meat separately.

RICE PUDDING *(grjónagrautur)*

70 g (2 1/2 oz) rice
4 dl (14 fl oz 1 3/4 cup) milk
4 dl (14 fl oz 1 3/4 cup) water
1/2 tsp salt
25 g (1 oz) raisins
3 tbsp sugar
1/4 tsp cinnamon

Wash the rice in cold water. Put the rice in boiling water with the salt. Boil for 15 minutes. Add the milk and the raisins and simmer for another 10-15 minutes. Stir well while boiling. Serve with cinnamon sugar.

SKYR

Skyr, a smooth curd made of skimmed milk, is a favourite food with Icelanders, especially eaten in the traditional fashion, with cream or milk and a little sugar. It is also delicious plain with fresh fruits. High in protein and almost devoid of fat, skyr is a healthy food, which adds a special flavour to many recipes. As a substitute for skyr, low-fat curd cheese can be used.

PANCAKES (pönnukökur)

130 g (4 1/2 oz) flour
6 dl (1 pt 2 5/8 cups) milk
3 eggs
1/2 tsp salt
1/2 tsp sugar
1/4 tsp vanilla essence
40 g margarine

Beat together eggs, milk and vanilla. Mix the dry ingredients. Add them to the egg mixture and blend thoroughly. Keep in a fridge for about 1 hour. Melt butter and whisk with the dough. Keep the pancake pan fairly hot, pour on the batter. Roll about to cover the pan and make the pancake thin. Bake for a moment, then turn it over and bake the other side for a short while. Transfer to a plate. Sprinkle with sugar or serve with jam and whipped cream.

CHRISTMAS CAKE (jólakaka)

150 g (5 oz) butter
150 g (5 oz) sugar
3 eggs
250 g (9 oz) flour
2 tsp baking powder
2 tsp cardamom
1 dl (3 1/2 fl oz 1/2 cup) milk
100 g raisins

Whisk together butter and sugar. Mix the dry ingredients and put half of it in the mixture. Add the milk and cardamom with the rest of the ingredients and the raisins. Place in an oblong cake mould and bake at 170°C (325°F) for 45 minutes.

RAX

Thorramatur

THORRAMATUR

According to the old almanac, the month of Thorri lasts from January 22 till February 24 and goes back to pagan ceremonies in Nordic countries. It was the custom to get together and celebrate Thorri, worship the ancient deities and drink to their health.Then food was served followed by dancing, singing and drinking until the break of day. Thorri is still celebrated today and popular all over Iceland. The people would not dream of giving up these midwinter festivities when the sun begins to rise again in the sky and the day gets longer. The Thorri celebrations are a typically Icelandic phenomenon preserved nowhere except in this country. The delicatessen counters of the food stores are groaning under the loaded Thorri dishes, reminding people that Thorri has come again. Entertainment is marked by tradition, people dance and sing national songs and many cannot do without having shark and an Icelandic schnapps (brennivín), maintaining that it is almost a panacea. Thorramatur is really the most national of everything national in Icelandic food: smoked lamb, shark, soured briskets of lamb, sheepheads, pressed meat, soured ram testicles, dried fish with butter, flatbread, cod maws......

RAM'S TESTICLES
(hrútspungar)
SHEEPHEAD
(svið)
HEAD CHEESE
(sviðasulta)
PICKLED LAMB
(bringukollar)
ROLLED MEAT
(lundabaggi)
SHARK
(hákarl)
LIVER SAUSAGE
(lifrarpylsa)
BLOOD PUDDING
(blóðmör)
FLAT BREAD
(flatkökur)
SMOKED LAMB
(hangikjöt)
DRIED FISH
(harðfiskur)